To a very special GRANDDAUGHTER

Written by Pam Brown
Illustrations by Juliette Clarke

Whatever anyone tells you
about wealth and success –
grandchildren are the very
best thing that can happen

EXLEY
MT. KISCO, NEW YORK • WATFORD,

IT'S WONDERFUL HAVING YOU

Most people fail in so many, many ways.
But when their grandchildren run into their arms,
none of the failures matter.

. . .

A granddaughter is the best excuse ever invented.
You can go anywhere, do anything, eat everything in
sight - just so long as you've a grandchild in tow.

. . .

When I wake up feeling old
and it's dark outside, and wet and cold
I *gloom* a little - and then I say
"Oh, never mind - today's the day
You come. I must get baking
and spreading jam and sandwich-making
- How glittering and bright the rain!"
And feel that I am young again.

. . .

A small part of me wants to call out, don't grow so fast. I scarcely got to know the three-year-old before you suddenly were seven. And *still* you sprout. But, the more there is of you, the more there is to love. And inside you are *all* the ages you have been. Never lost. Just set aside so you can grow more beautiful and wise.

. . .

Every year I have to live has become doubly valuable since you came into this world.

. . .

The hands of little children have bones as delicate as a bird's - and they fit into a grandparent's grasp as snugly as a bird into its nest.

. . .

There comes a day,
when all the kids are grown and gone
and life has taken on a hint of grey
and it's a little dull,
that someone calls you up to say
- with all the glee
of one who's handing you a huge bouquet
- "Start knitting, Grandma!"

And at that very second, every hint of rain
is blown away.
The sun comes out
and life begins again.

. . .

Here she comes, luminous with pride, on her feet and moving. She stops, lurches, collapses neatly. Beams. Reorganizes. Up again. Come *on*, now - you can do it! And she does - standing, rocking slightly, clutching at your knees.

I really think that deserves a jelly bean. And a kiss.

. . .

I thought I had forgotten all I ever knew about babies, but see, my arms remembered.

. . .

LIFE BEGINS AGAIN

In life there are no
second chances - save through
one's grandchildren.

. . .

People getting older look back and
sigh a little. Then come the
grandchildren - and the future
opens up again.

. . .

When all the other loves
have grown old, a new
love comes to see one
through the winter years.
One's grandchildren.

. . .

The coming of a grandchild pushes one further back along the generations. Suddenly one is aware of time passing - of the brevity of one's existence. And yet - here is something new to live for. Here is someone who will lead one into new discoveries. Here is a new beginning.

. . .

I have danced so long - danced and laughed and loved, to different tunes and paces, and now am growing a little tired, a little slower in my steps. But now I see you coming on to the floor, eager to begin. We will dance together for a while - and I will remember the days when I, too, was young.

. . .

Just when I thought life was running down for me, you came along - and now each day is a new astonishment.

. . .

STICKY, NOISY AND MUDDY ...

Grandchildren love to help.

They harvest your peas. Early.

They rip out tomato shoots. The flowering ones.

They weed. The onions.

They seed the lawn. And so delight the birds.

They bring you bunches of flowers. Gathered from the roots.

And smile. And say "I *luf* you, Grandma."

And you smile back - and say you love them too.

And you do - you really do.

. . .

A grandchild under eight is invariably sticky.

- But what's a touch of sticky between friends?

. . .

Grandchildren can undo, wriggle through, squash under and climb over any barrier in their path. That is why most grandparents have white hair.

. . .

Someone could make a fortune by inventing a device for muffling granddaughter squawks.

. . .

A granddaughter can exhaust you, aggravate you, eat you out of house and home - but then she clambers bonily on to your knee, clasps buttery fingers around your neck, plants raspberry-tasting kisses on your face and says, "I *do* love it here!" And who *cares* if there's mud and wet leaves clear through the entire house?

. . .

TIME FOR YOU

Grandparents have time to listen, time to tell you stories and time to go down to the bottom of the garden and see what you have discovered.

. . .

Once, when my own children were small, I was always on my way somewhere, and against the clock. And then, at long last, I had time to hold your little hand and stare into workmen's trenches, or up at festival lights, time to stand on bridges and watch for the 12:15 train, time to kick falling leaves and splash in puddles, time to listen to a Vivaldi concerto, time to talk to every cat that strolls to meet you along its garden wall.

That's what I feel grandparents are for.

. . .

Grandads and grandmas are not that much wiser than other people. The best things we can do for you is to be there when you need us. Always.

. . .

SHARING WONDERS

For you the world is new-minted.
And "Come and see! Come and see!" is an
instruction to me to rediscover long lost marvels.

. . .

I have watched the world in your face - seeing it
transformed by wonderment and joy.
Your first old-fashioned carousel, your first
encounter with Mozart, your first chance meeting
with a deer, your first discovery of piebald rats, your
first sight of the sea, your first grand dining out,
your first....
Thank you for all of these things, my dearest.
The brightness had all faded, the music blurred - but
you brought everything to vivid life again.

. . .

Hold my hand and I will take you to the places where my mother took me when I was very small, and where I took your parents when they were small as you. We will see tree cathedrals, hear beautiful music and I will watch your face shine with new discoveries - just as I once watched theirs. And as my grandmother watched my own.

. . .

Two noses against the glass of the display case. A grandparent and a grandchild making discoveries together.

. . .

Look up. There is the
endlessness of space - the
great stars made of fire and
ice, wide silver rivers flung
across the sky....
And here you are, holding
my hand - watching,
considering, alive. More
wonderful than all that wide
immensity.
My dear. My love.
My granddaughter.

. . .

MY SPECIAL PERSON

You are unique. One in a million, million. And do you know that I love you as though you were the only granddaughter that ever existed.

. . .

How did I come to have a granddaughter so beautiful, so clever, so wise, so kind and loving and so concerned for others?

So unexpected. So full of curiosity. So inventive. And at times so baffling, so exasperating, so downright maddening.

What mix of genes made a beginning for the complexity of you?

. . .

Granddaughters are not often like the granddaughters in story books - perpetually happy and loving and helpful and clever and good.

You are a lot better. You spring surprises!

. . .

SO FAR FROM YOU

Far-away grandparents write and call - but how they ache when they are told of your clear round, or your sandcastle by the sea, or your solo, or your being Mary in the Christmas play.

They ask about it. They imagine it.

But the moment is gone and you are moving on, getting older, growing taller, trying something new.

And we live too far away.

We love you so much. Our thoughts are with you whatever you do.

We just wish and wish that we could follow our thoughts sometimes.

. . .

It is very difficult to cram love into a package - but long-distance grandparents try.

. . .

Very small granddaughters like to use the telephone.
They just don't use it like other people.
They show you their bears.

. . .

Grandmas like phone calls that say;
"It's a little girl...."
"She smiled at me! 4:30 this morning!"
"She's sitting up and she's got a tooth."
"She took a step at lunchtime."
"She wants to speak to you."
"Grandma, when can you come and stay?"
"Grandma, I got an 'A' for physics. So I can do the engineering course."
"Grandma, can I bring him round?"
"Grandma, guess what? We're getting married!"

. . .

ON YOUR SIDE

Never forget, my lovely, grandparents may not be rich or all-wise or be able to change your mother's mind - but they love you and will do their very, very best to make things come right for you.

. . .

I'm on your side - whatever you want to be - an airline pilot or a dentist or a vet or a bus driver. Just as long as it's worth doing - and you put into it everything you've got.

. . .

Grandfathers and grandmothers are grandfathers and grandmothers, not people. So you can tell them anything.

. . .

A granddaughter is someone who needs a place to think, to unravel her problems, to plan, to cry, to dream.

And good grandparents have just such a corner in their houses.

. . .

Don't forget. Whatever the trouble, a grandma's and grandpa's arms are always open.

. . .

Thank you for all the joys that you have given me.
The first sight of your little, perfect hands.
Your first glad smile of recognition.
Your first tip-tilting steps into the safety of my arms.
All the wise and funny things you had to say.
All the dazzling, unexpected gifts of pebbles and dandelions, earthworms and earwigs, fluff-covered toffees, drawings and kisses.
All the secrets shared.
All the triumphs, big and small.
All the muddles brought for me to unravel.
Marvels of discovery - and love.
Tales of adventure,

of journeys, friendships and astonishments.

Accounts of troubles overcome,

of lessons learned.

Courage in disappointment and in loss.

Grim-faced determination.

Laughter. Lovely silliness.

All you have let me share.

It was worth waiting for - this overlapping

of our lives.

I'll treasure all of it until we're forced to part.

And then I'll travel on in great content

- carrying with me all the love you gave.

. . .

I WISH YOU...

Grandparents dream for their grandchildren all the things they hoped to have and missed - and all the things that gave them joy. They may not be the things you want - your dreams may be different. And so I wish you your own particular pleasures and discoveries and wonders - dreams tailor-made to fit your mind, loves tailor-made to fit your heart. Hold them gently, less they spoil. And if they pass, then let them go with only a small sigh. Sometimes you have to lose joys in order to make room for greater ones.

. . .

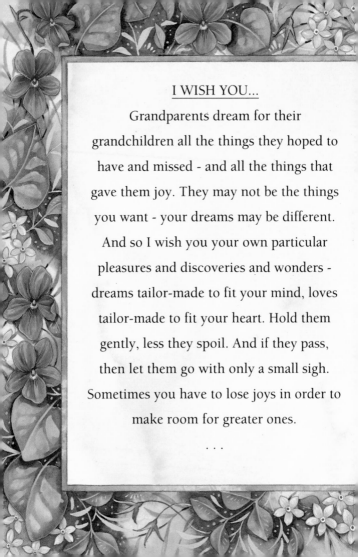

I wish that I could take all pain and loss and fear and failure from your life. But that is foolishness. For then - how could you learn? How could you grow?
I wish you, instead, courage to face such things - and wisdom to learn from them.

. . .

It is one of the saddest things in the world to see you discovering that the world can be unjust and cruel.
All I can do is to show you that it can also be exciting and beautiful and that there is always a moment of unexpected, shining, loving kindness.

. . .

HOPES FOR YOUR FUTURE

I hug myself to think of all that awaits you. Mountains and forests, lakes and oceans, a million creatures to astound and delight you. And a treasure house of things that those who have gone before have fashioned for you. Books and poems, monuments and paintings, music of every sort. How rich you are.

An heiress to all the wealth of Time.

. . .

Like every grandparent, I sometimes sigh for the things I never managed to do in life. But then I think of your hopes for the future. And smile.

. . .

There are so many places I have never seen, so many adventures that never came my way, so much music that I never heard, so many books I never discovered.

I hope you find them. And some part of me will share your joy.

. . .

Take with you into your future all my love. All the things we've seen together, all the music we have heard, all the people we have met and loved, all the secrets, all the gigglings, all the mischiefs we have made. I'll come with you as far as I'm allowed along your road - and when we part you'll take with you my hopes and half my heart.

. . .